HELLO
my name is
BLACK BOOK

A Graffiti Coloring Book by: Malcolm Williams AKA King Zoc 5

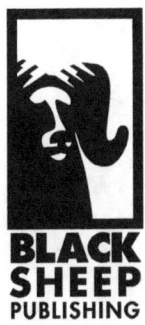

BLACK SHEEP PUBLISHING

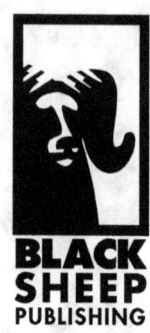

BLACK SHEEP PUBLISHING

BlackSheep Media Inc.
Black Book a Graffiti Coloring Book
Published through LULU.COM and
D. B. A. BlackSheep Publishing
A subsidiary of BlackSheep Media Inc.

Printed by U.S.A. .LULU.COM

Black Book: A Graffiti Coloring Book
Drawn, illustrated, outlined and
written by Malcolm Williams
AKA King ZOC 5

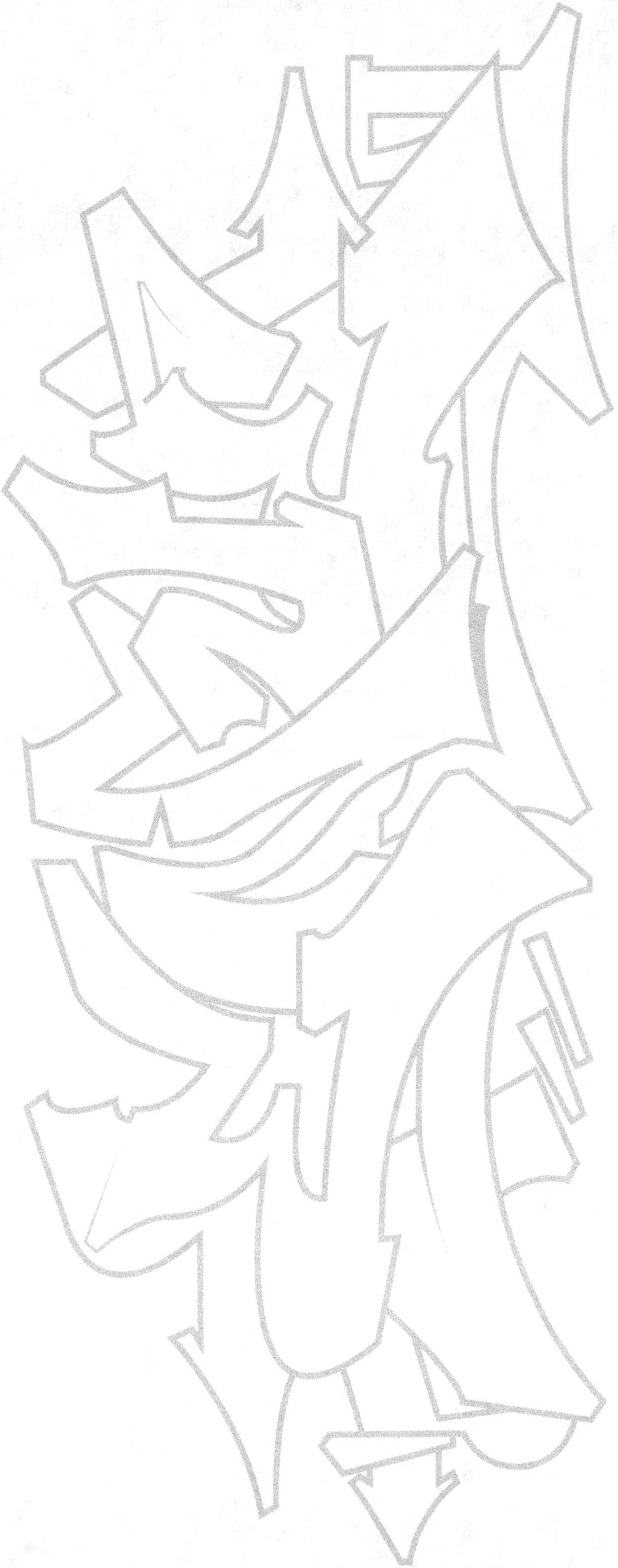

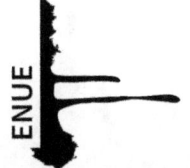
ENUE

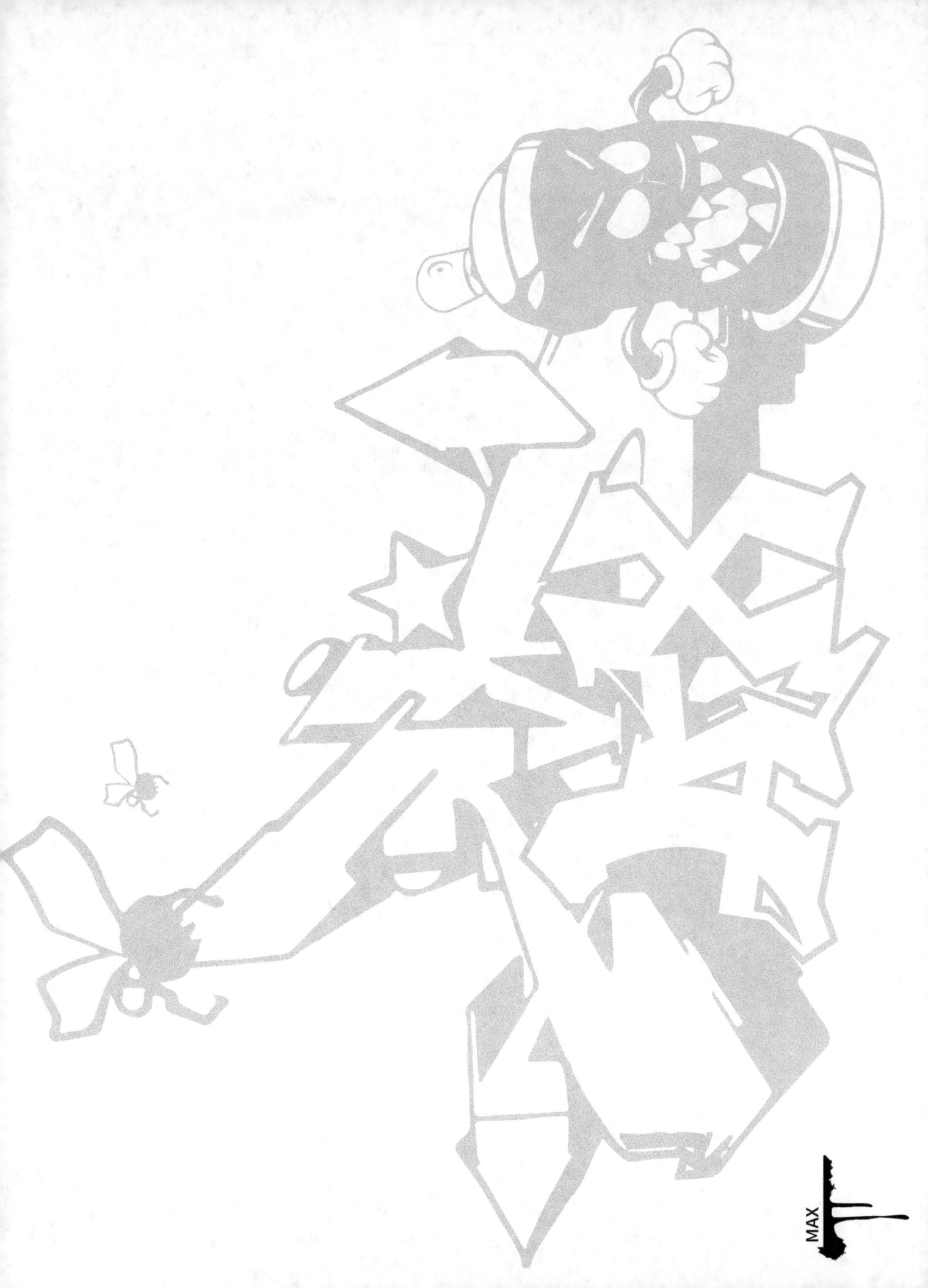

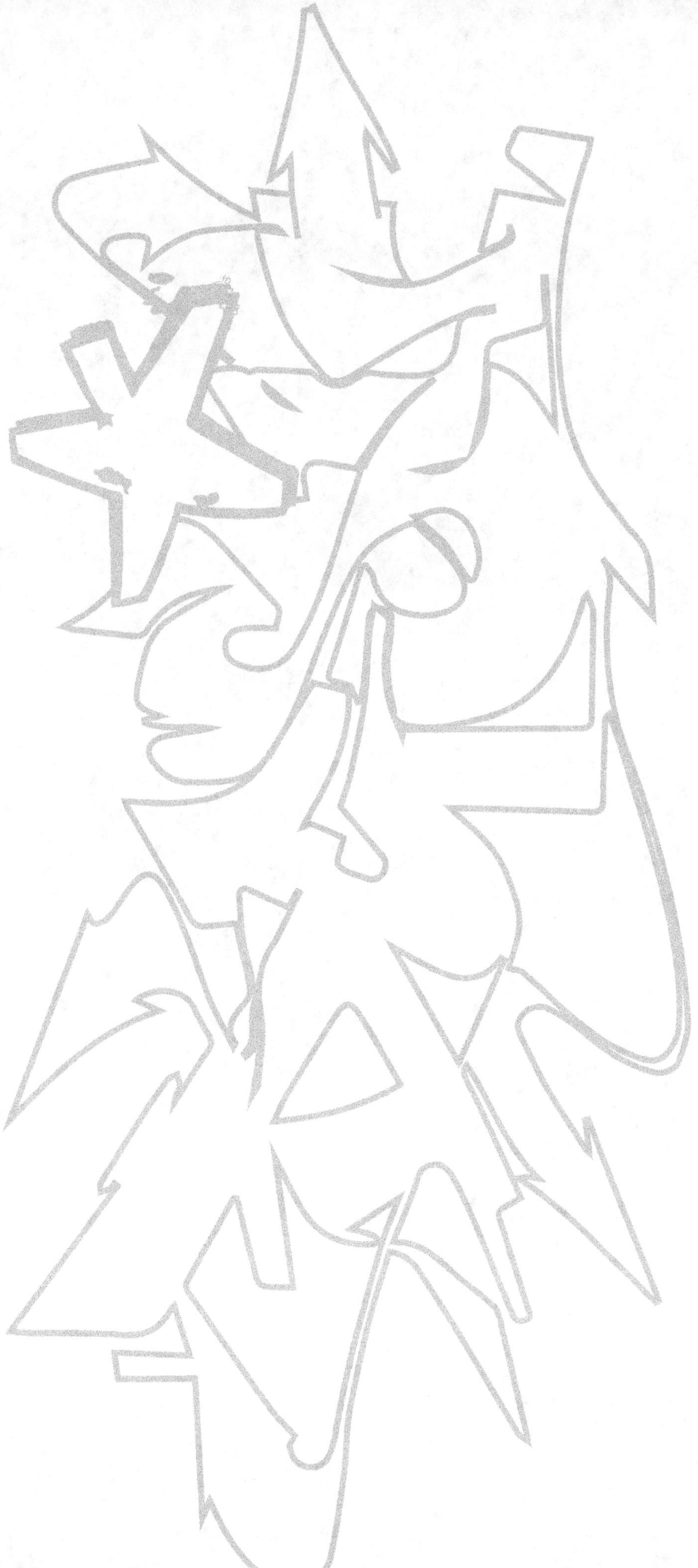

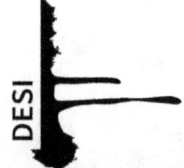

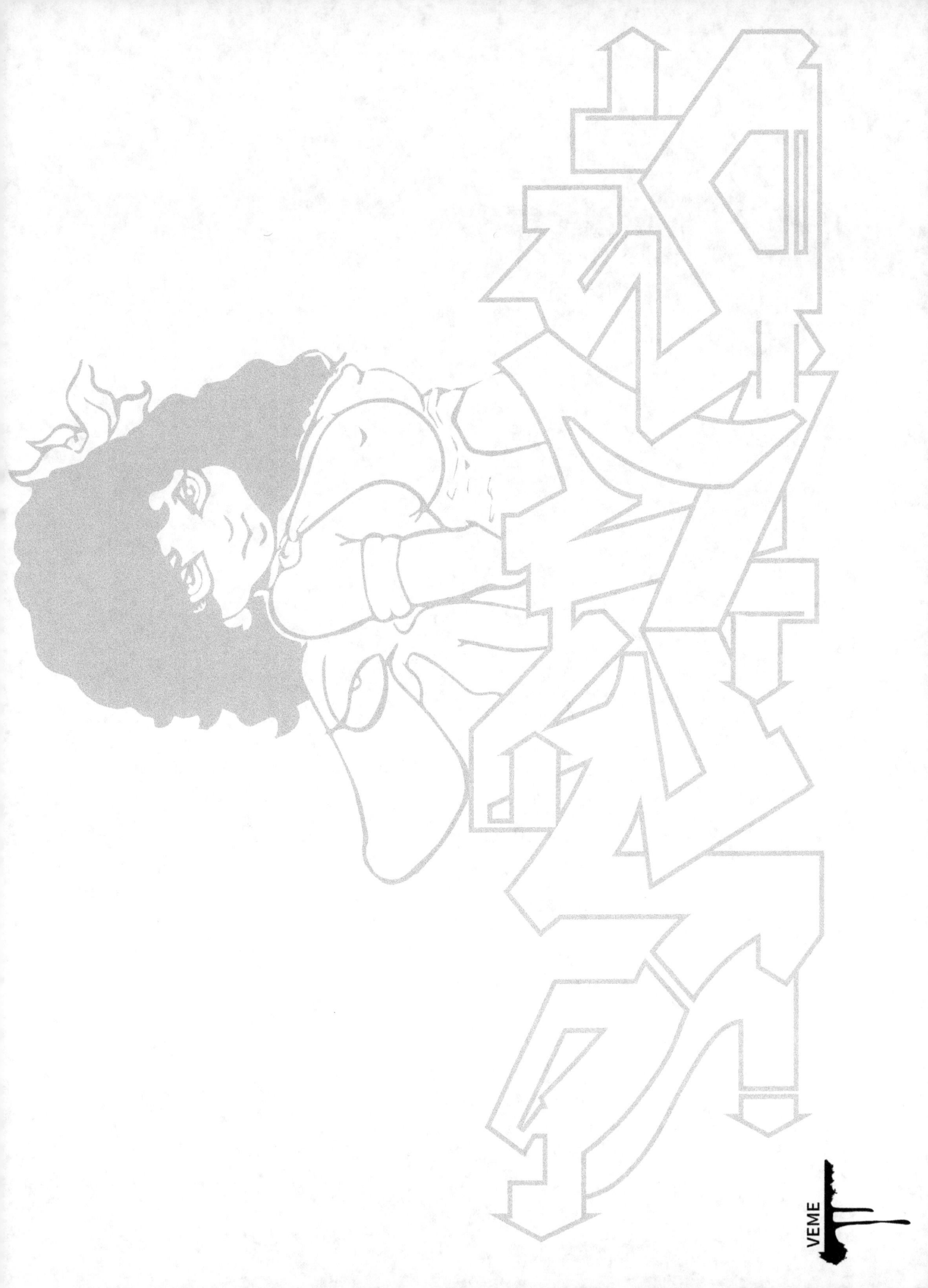

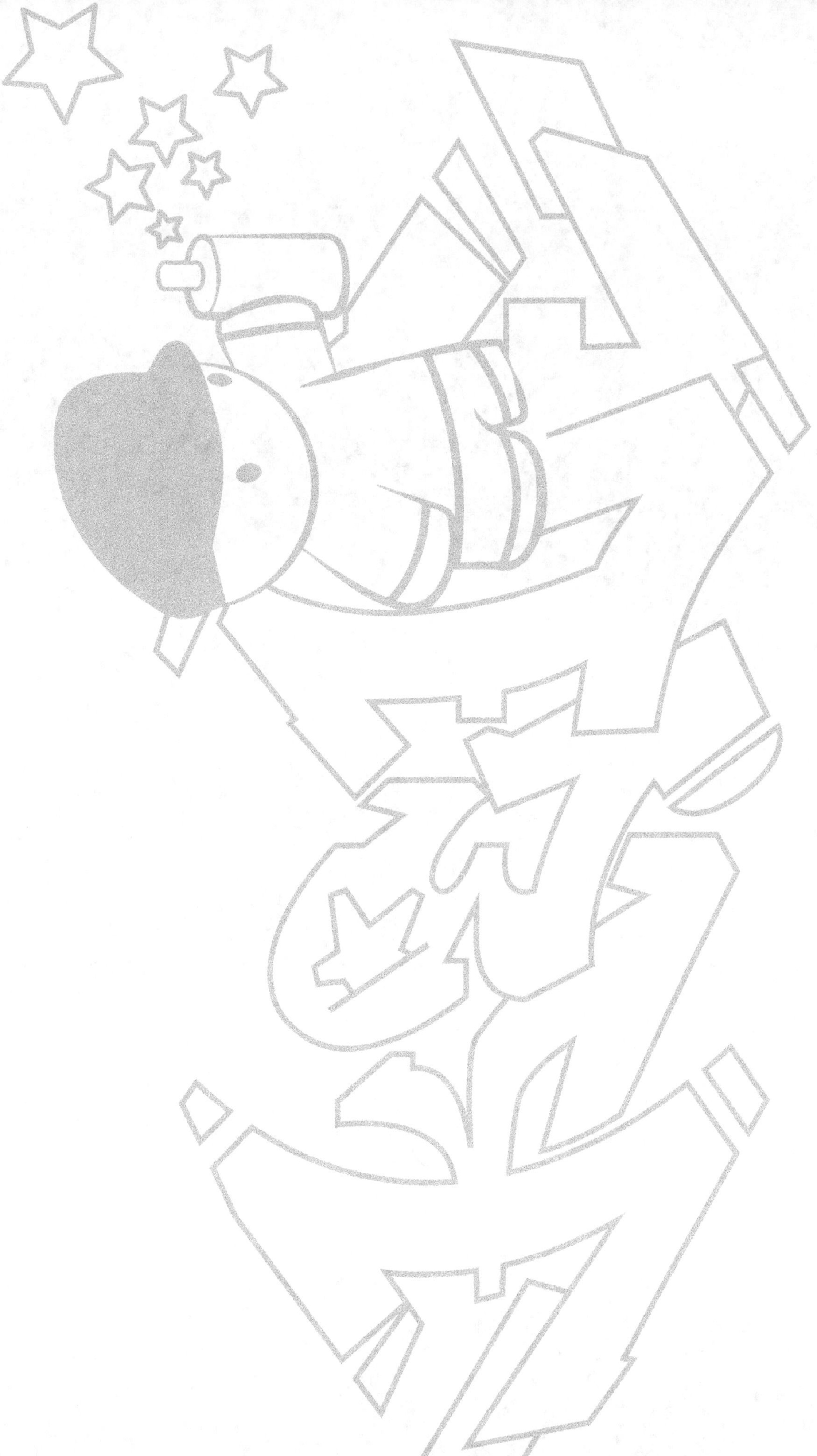

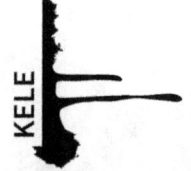

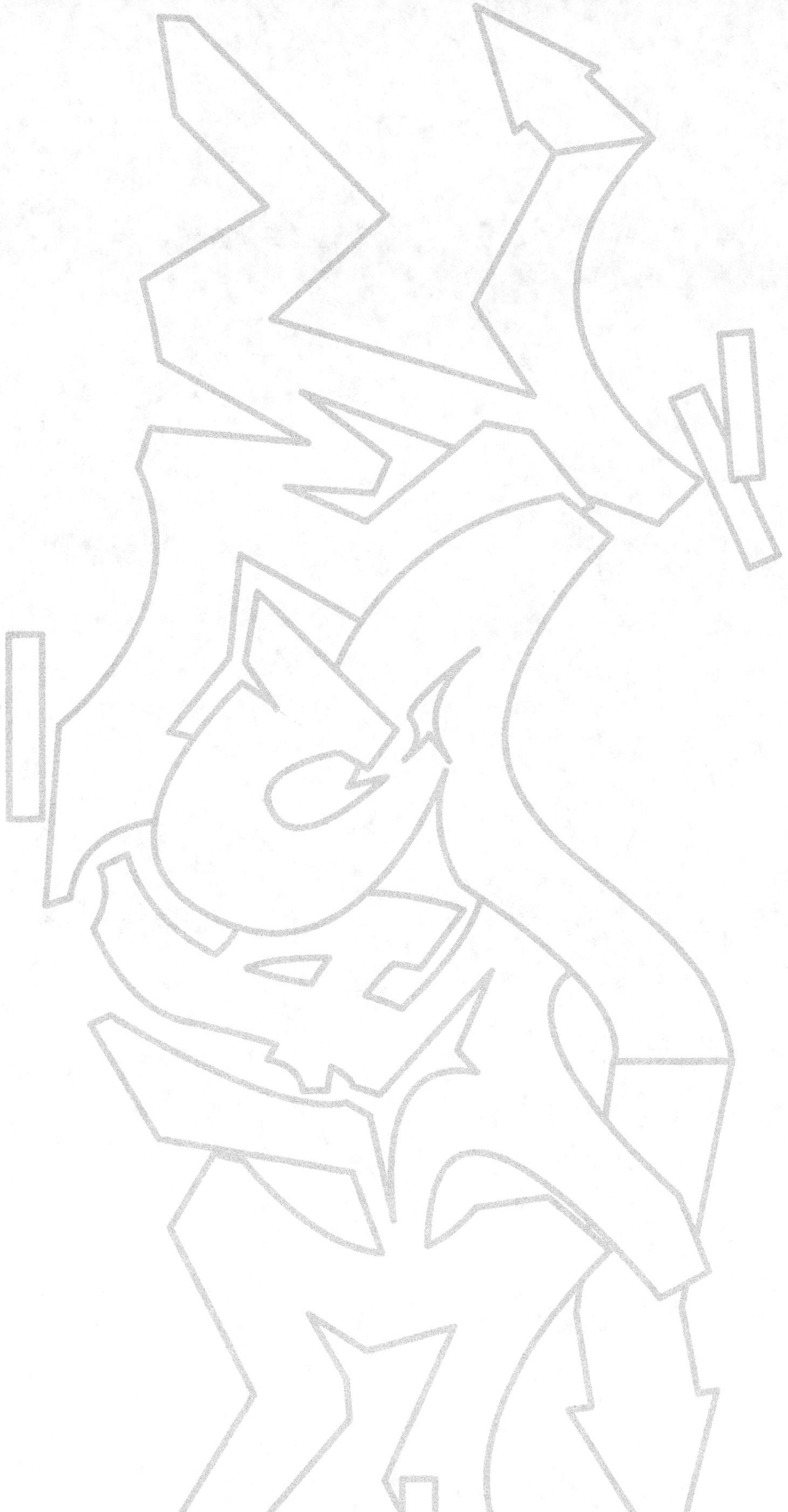

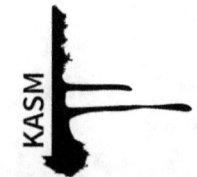

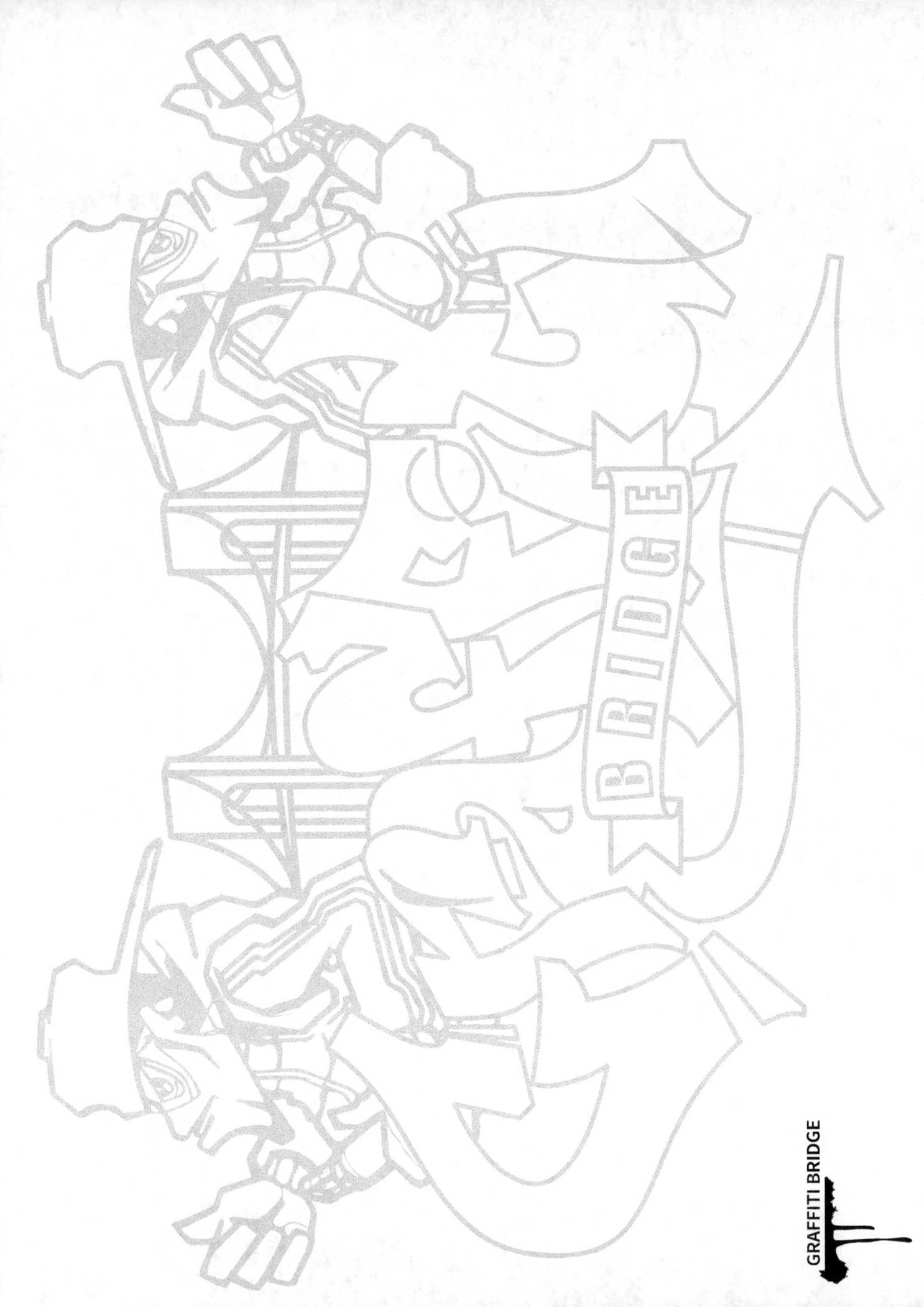

GRAFFITI BRIDGE

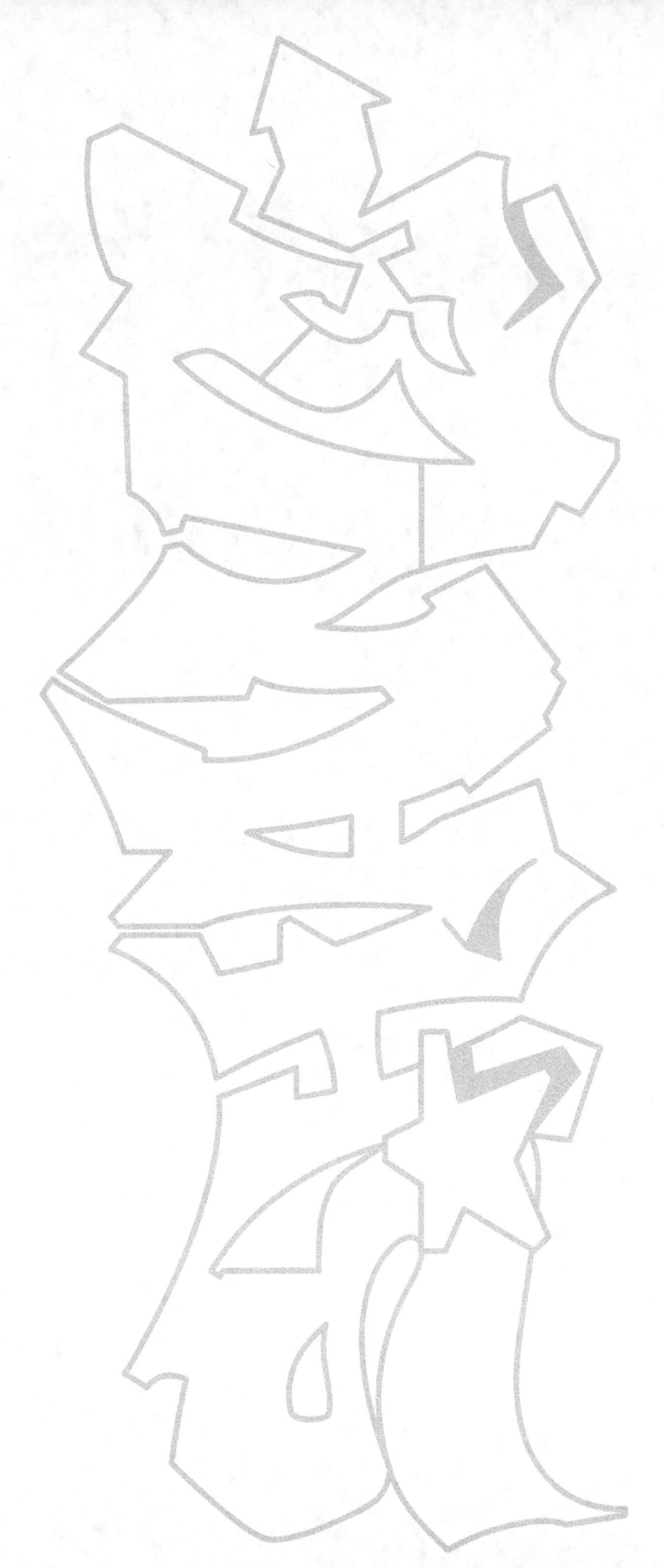

SHANE

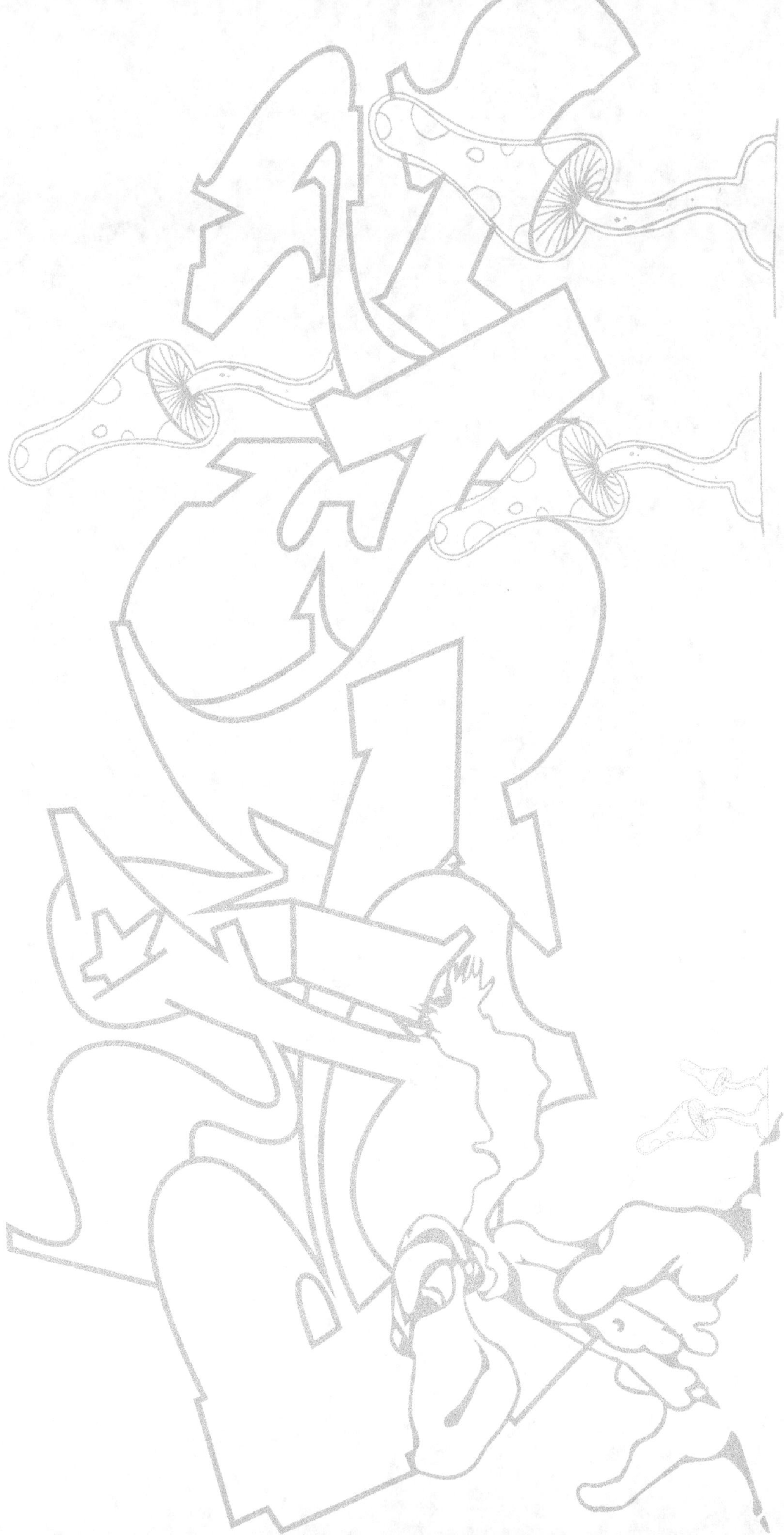

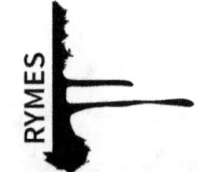
RYMES

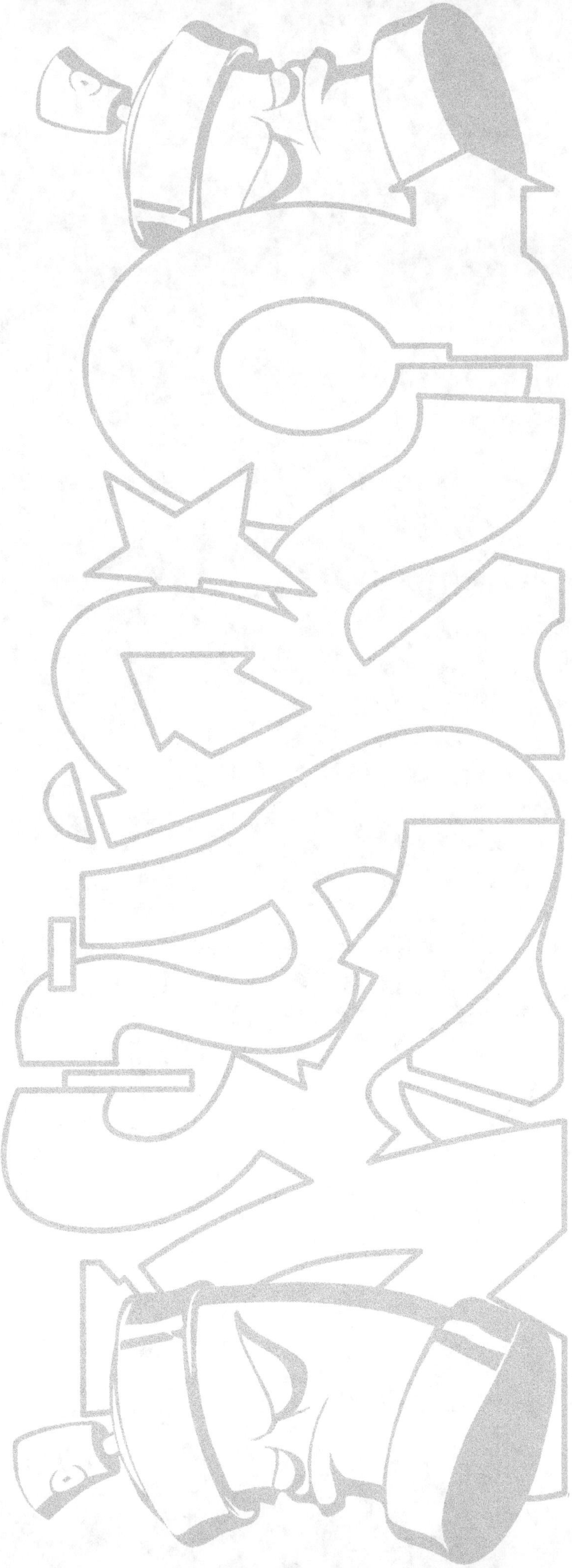

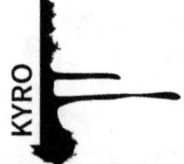

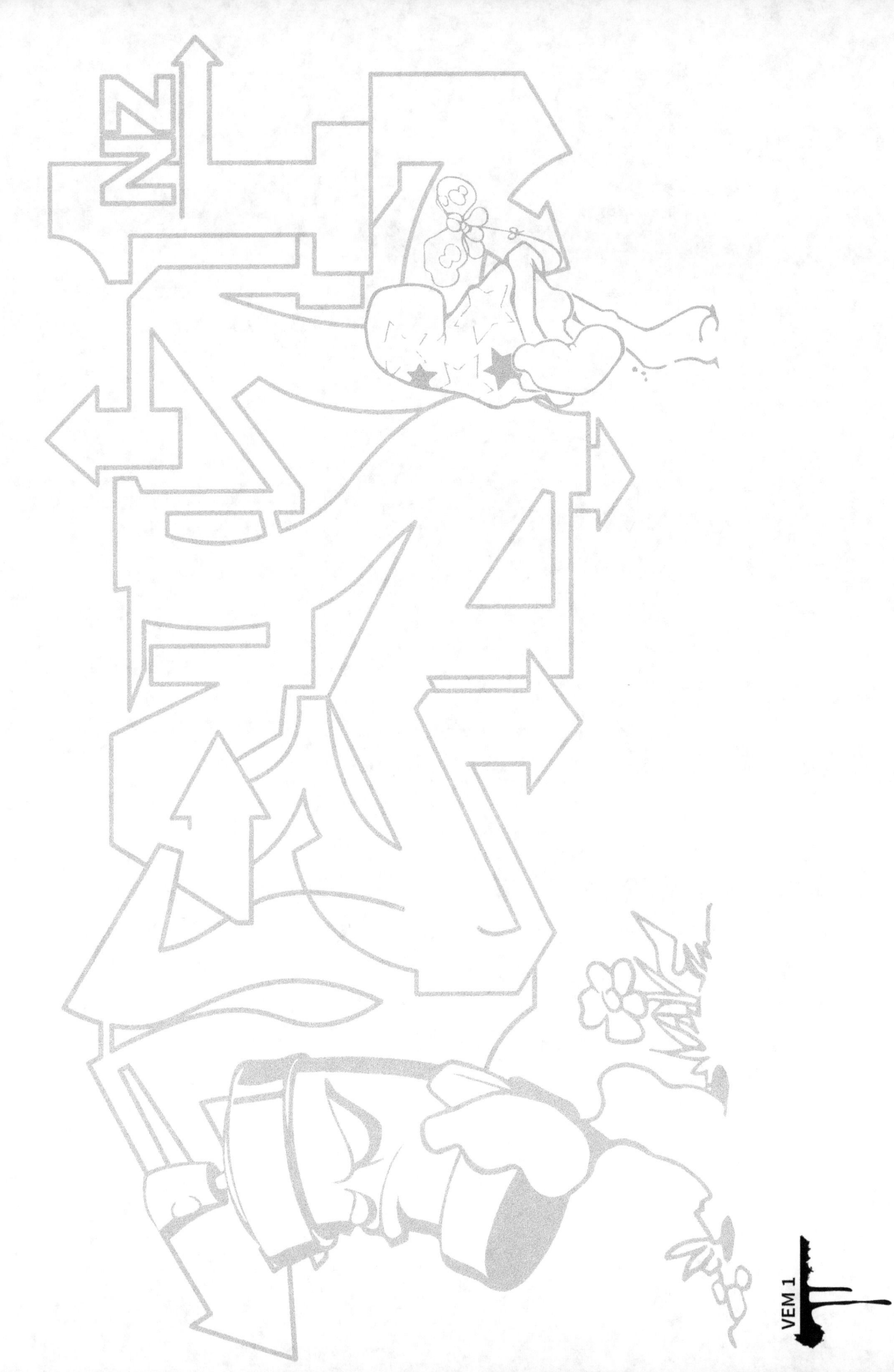

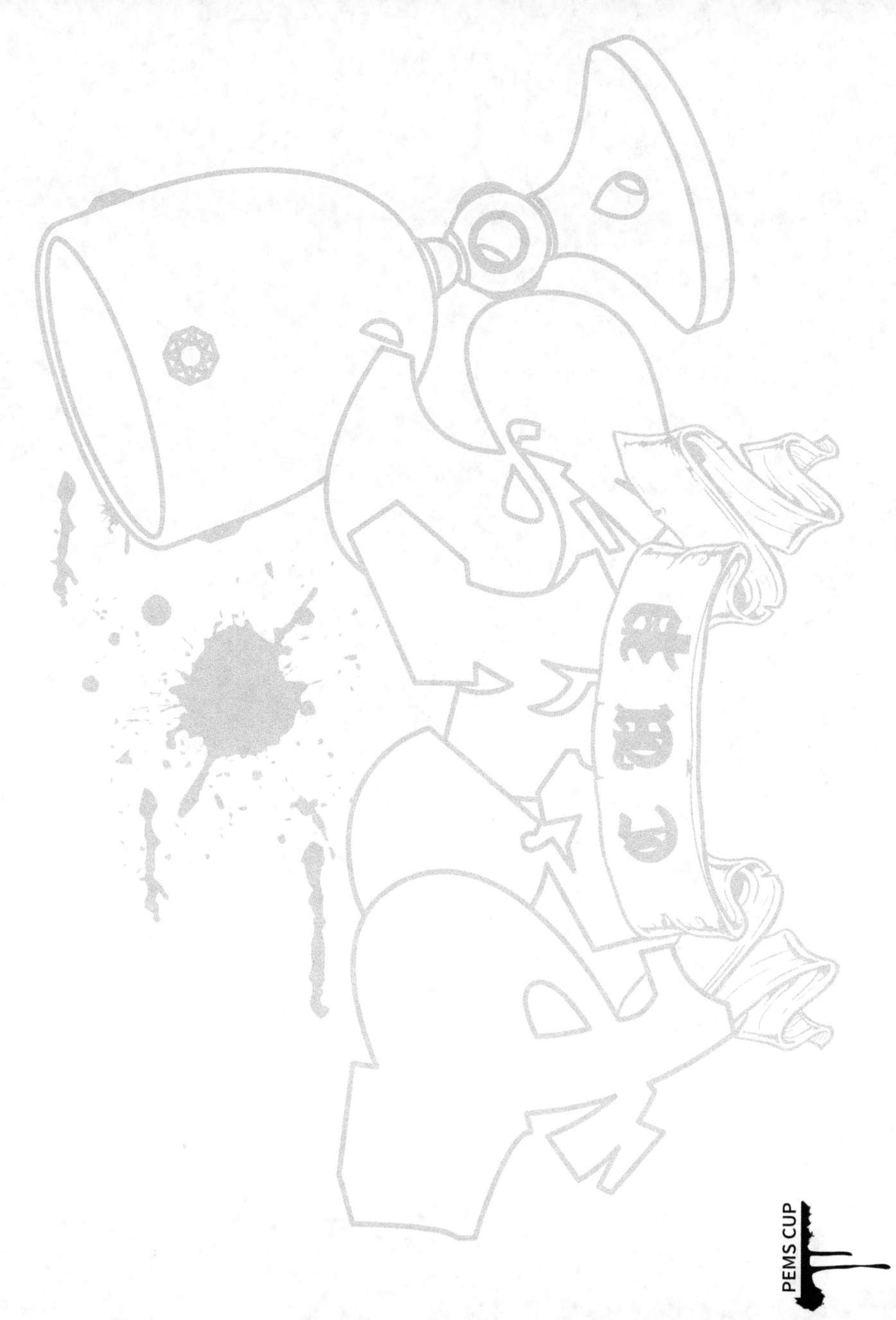

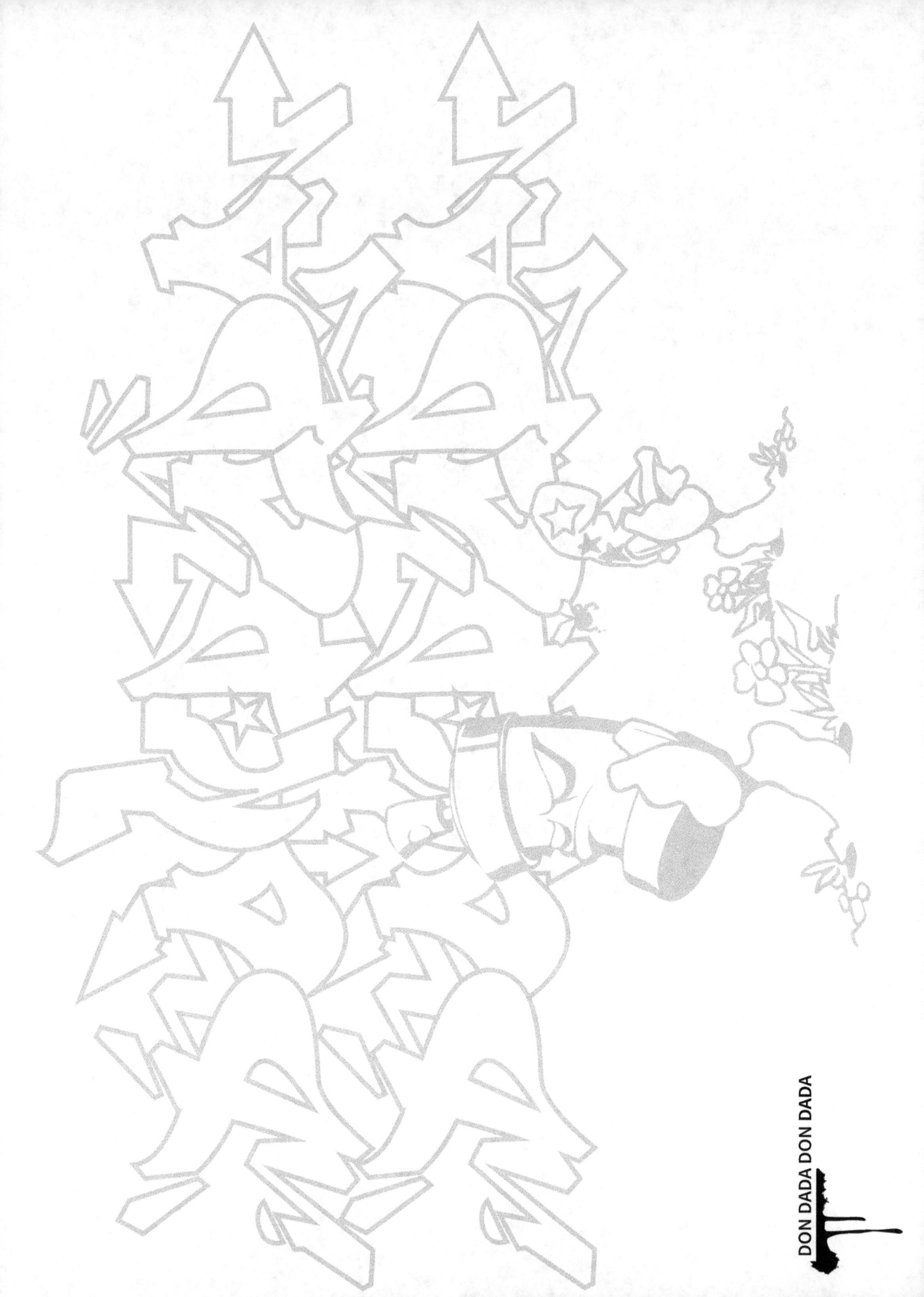

DON DADA DON DADA

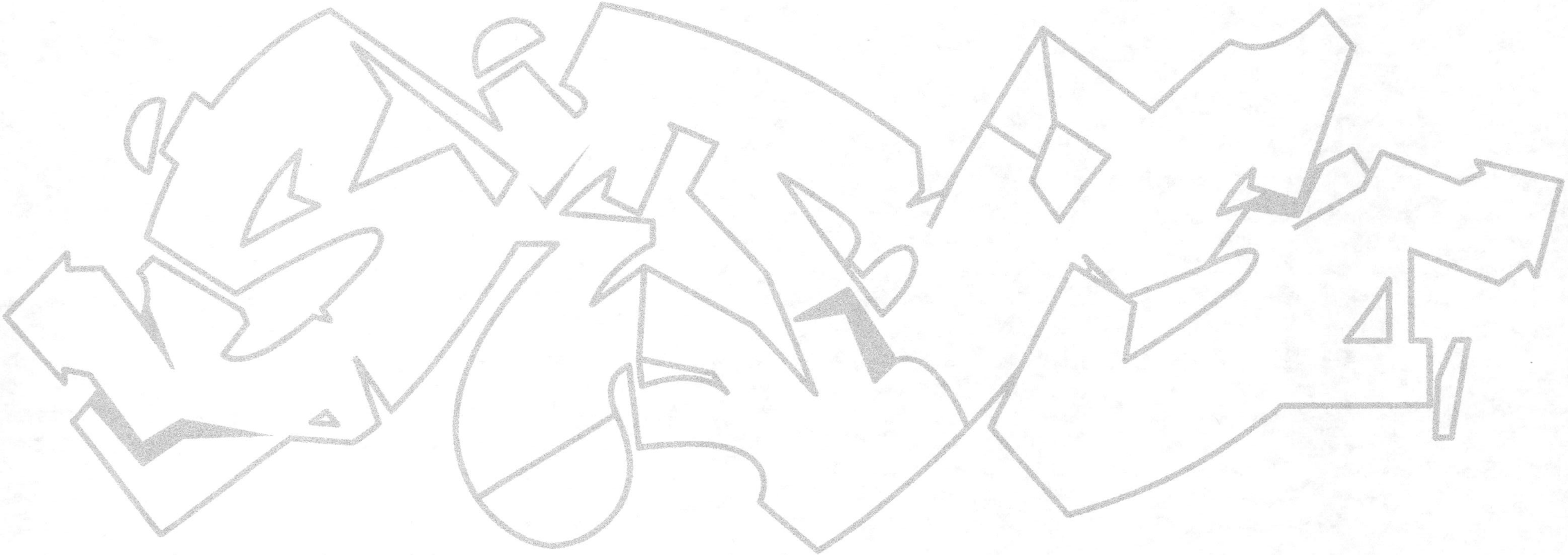

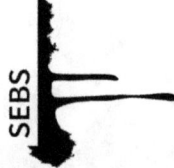

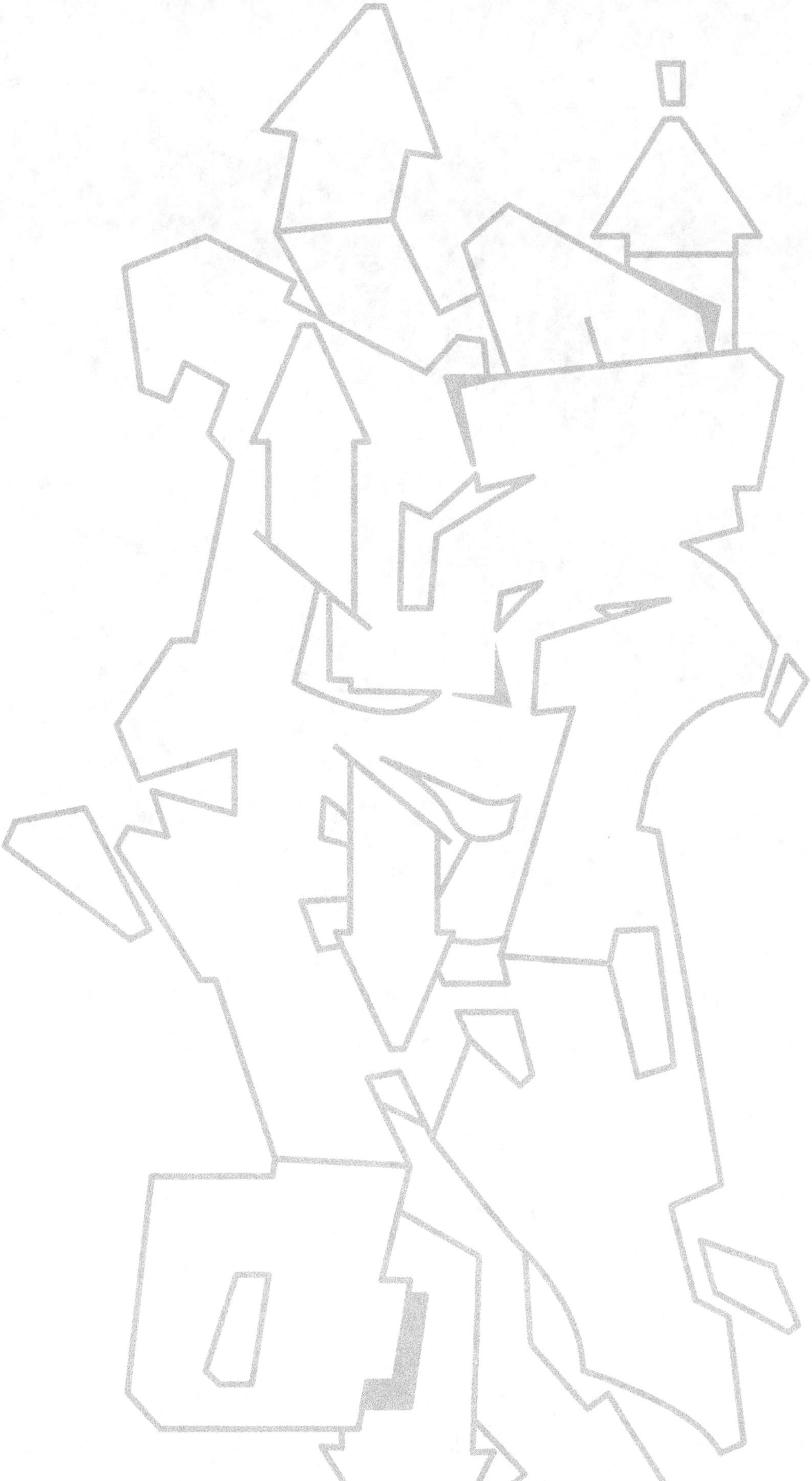

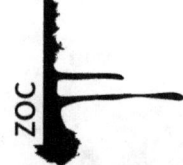

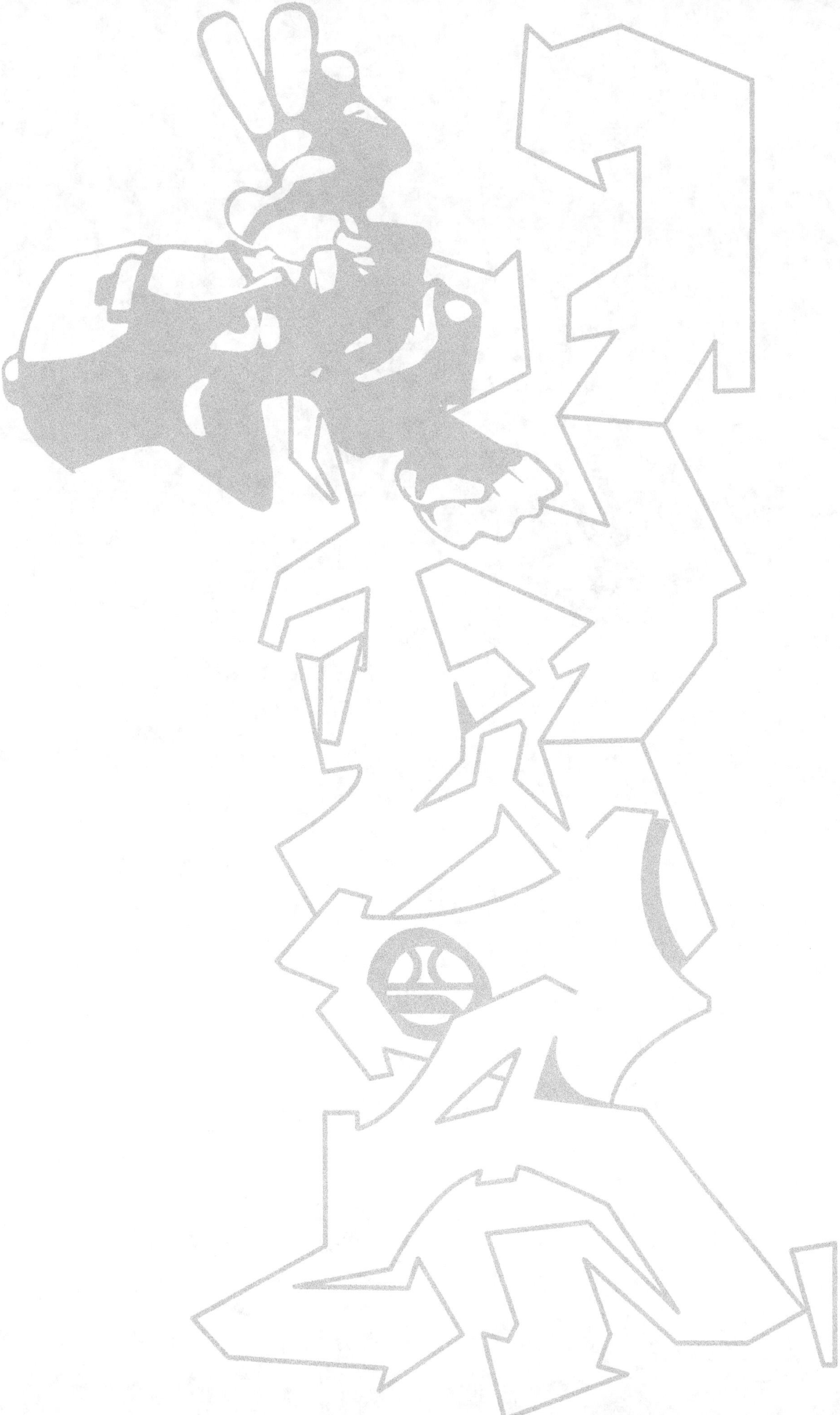

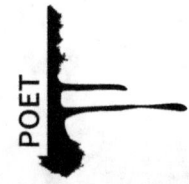

POET

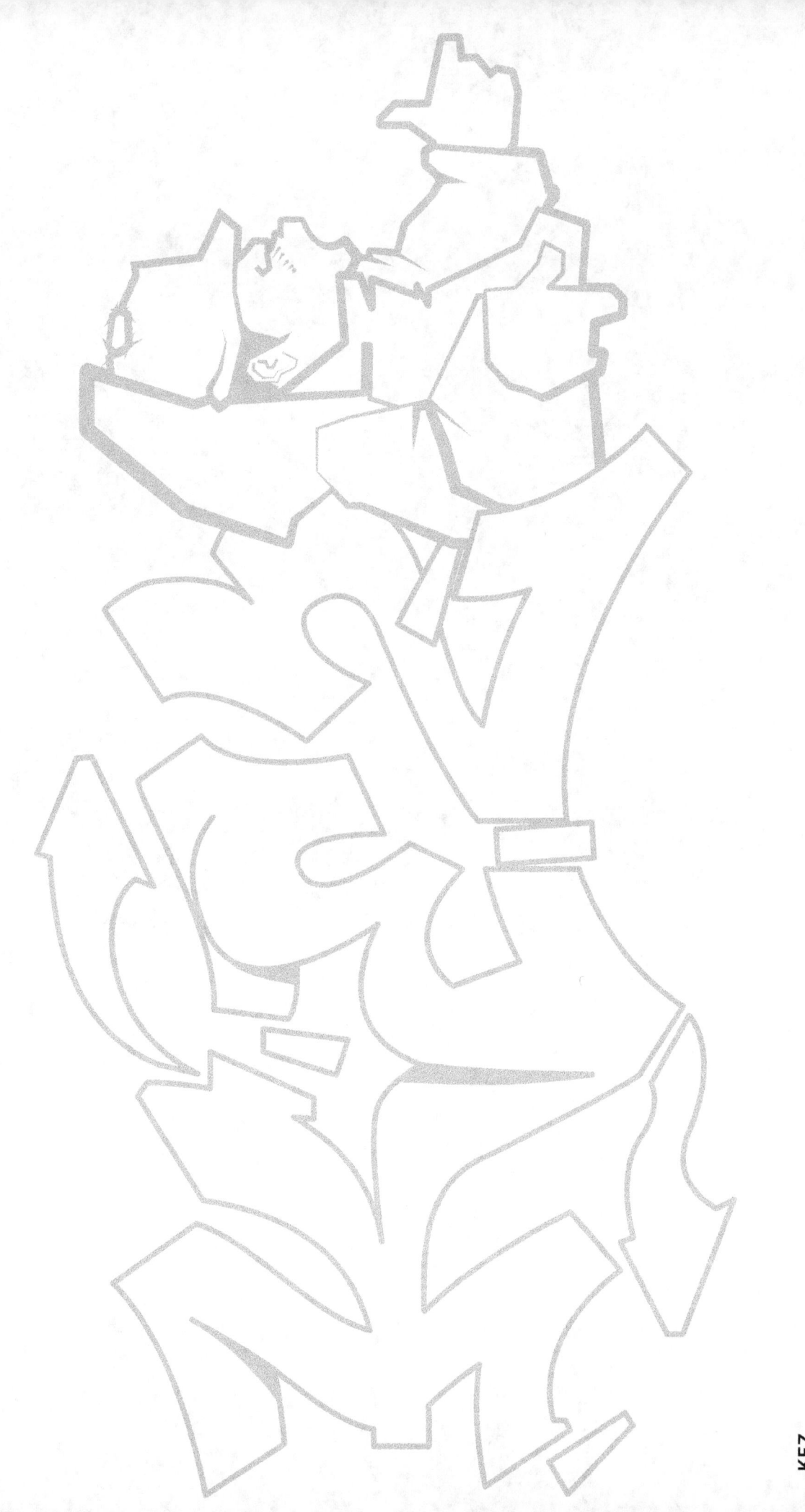

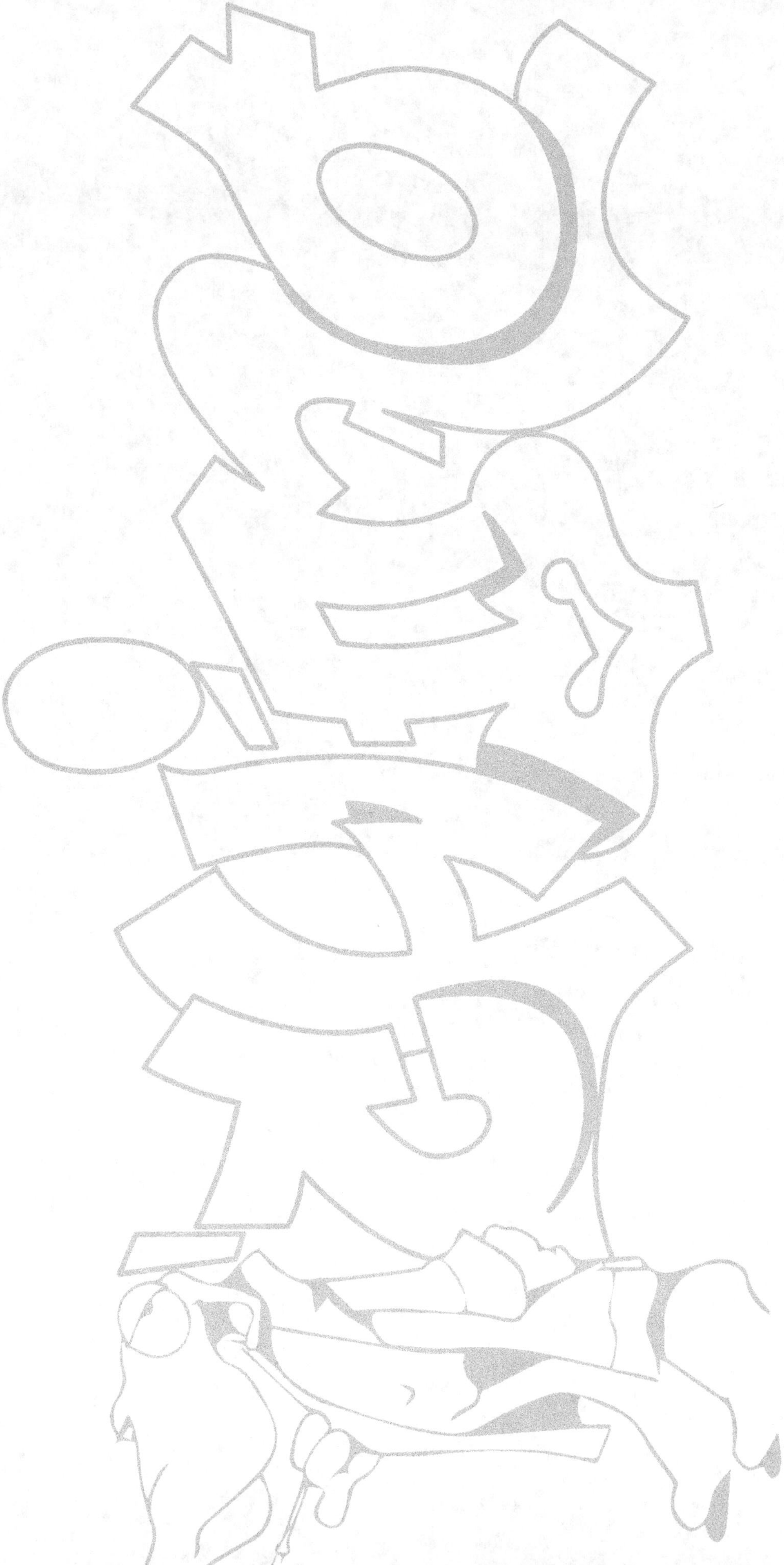

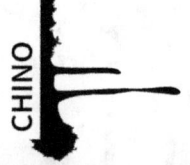

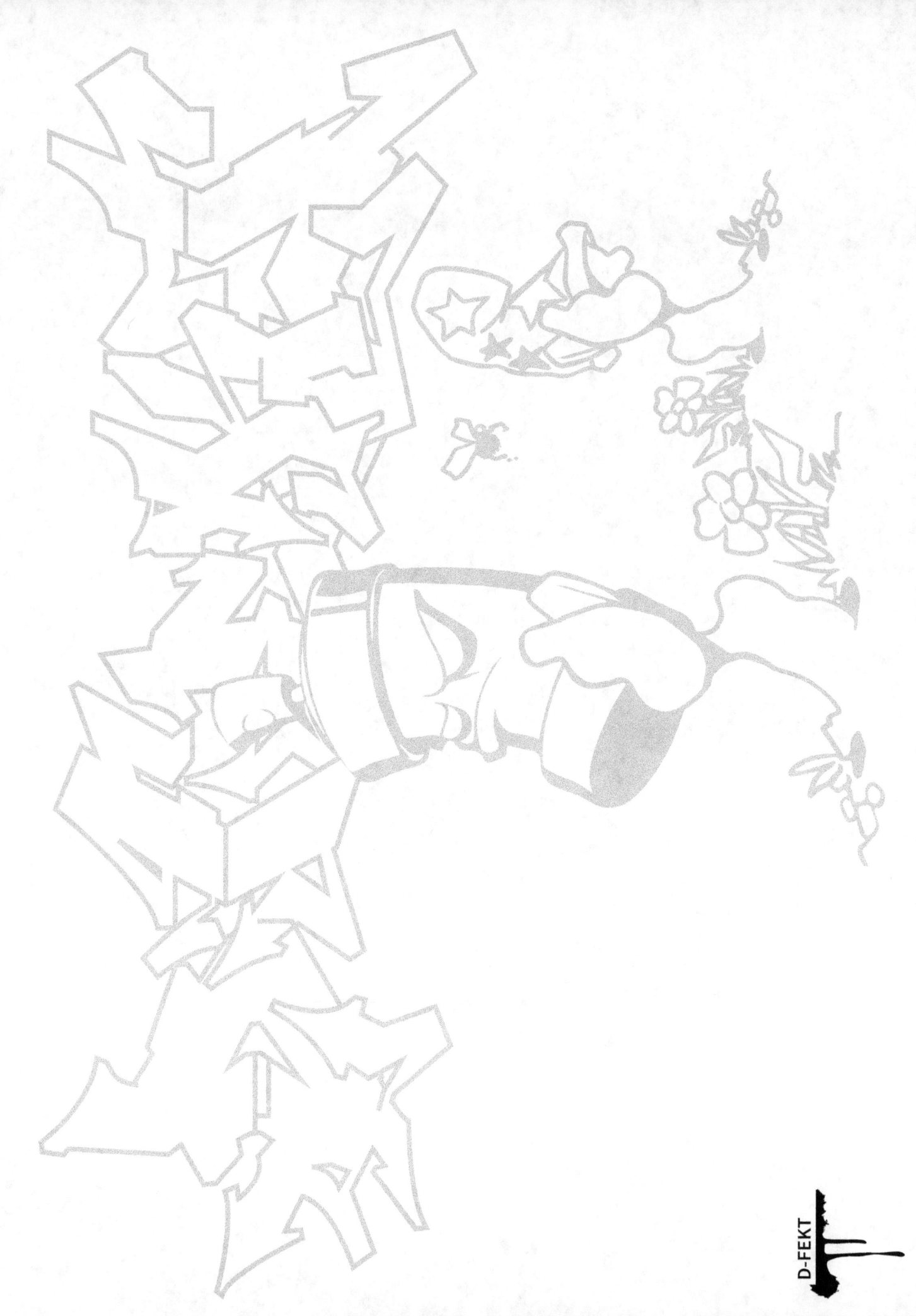

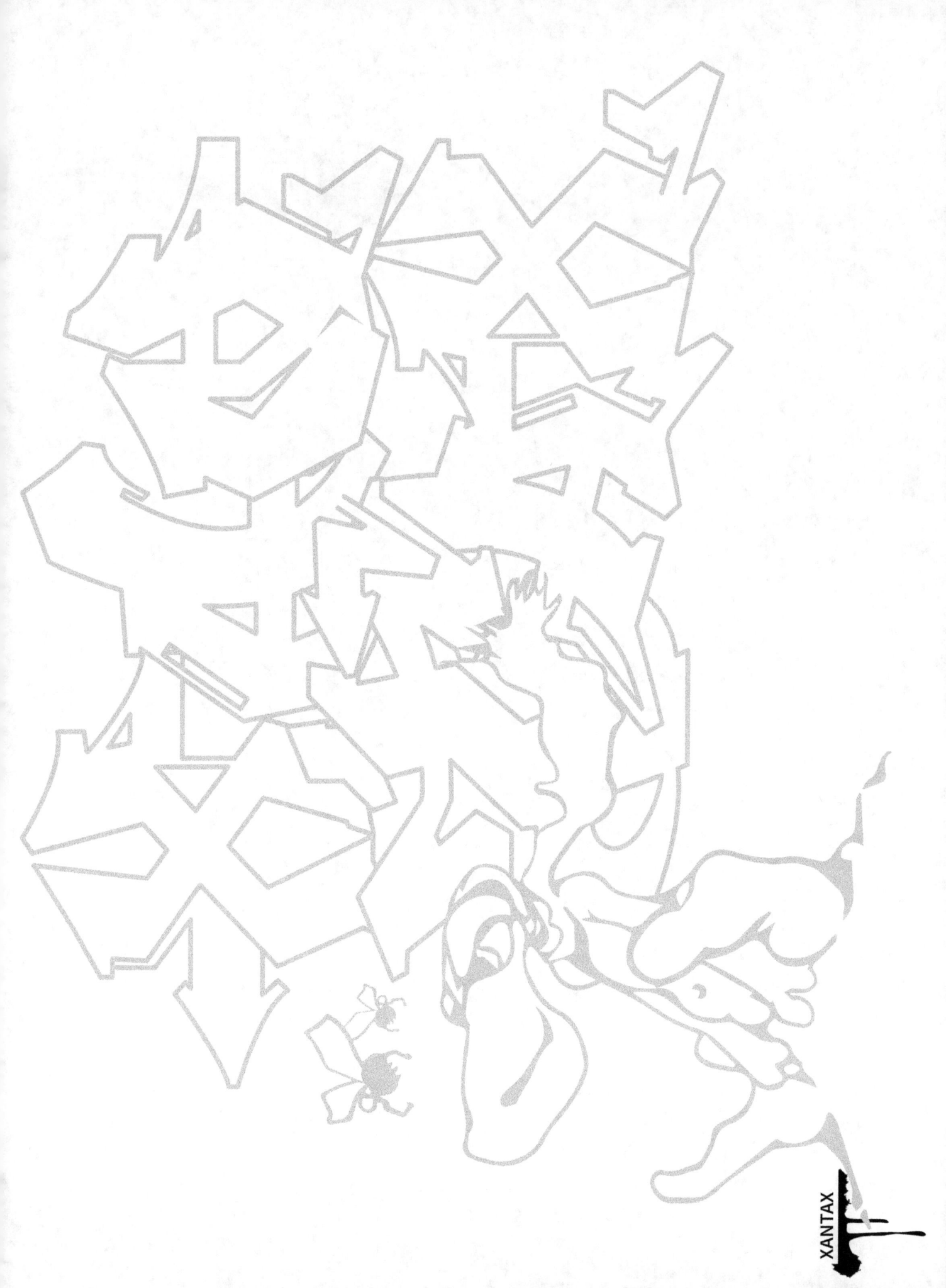

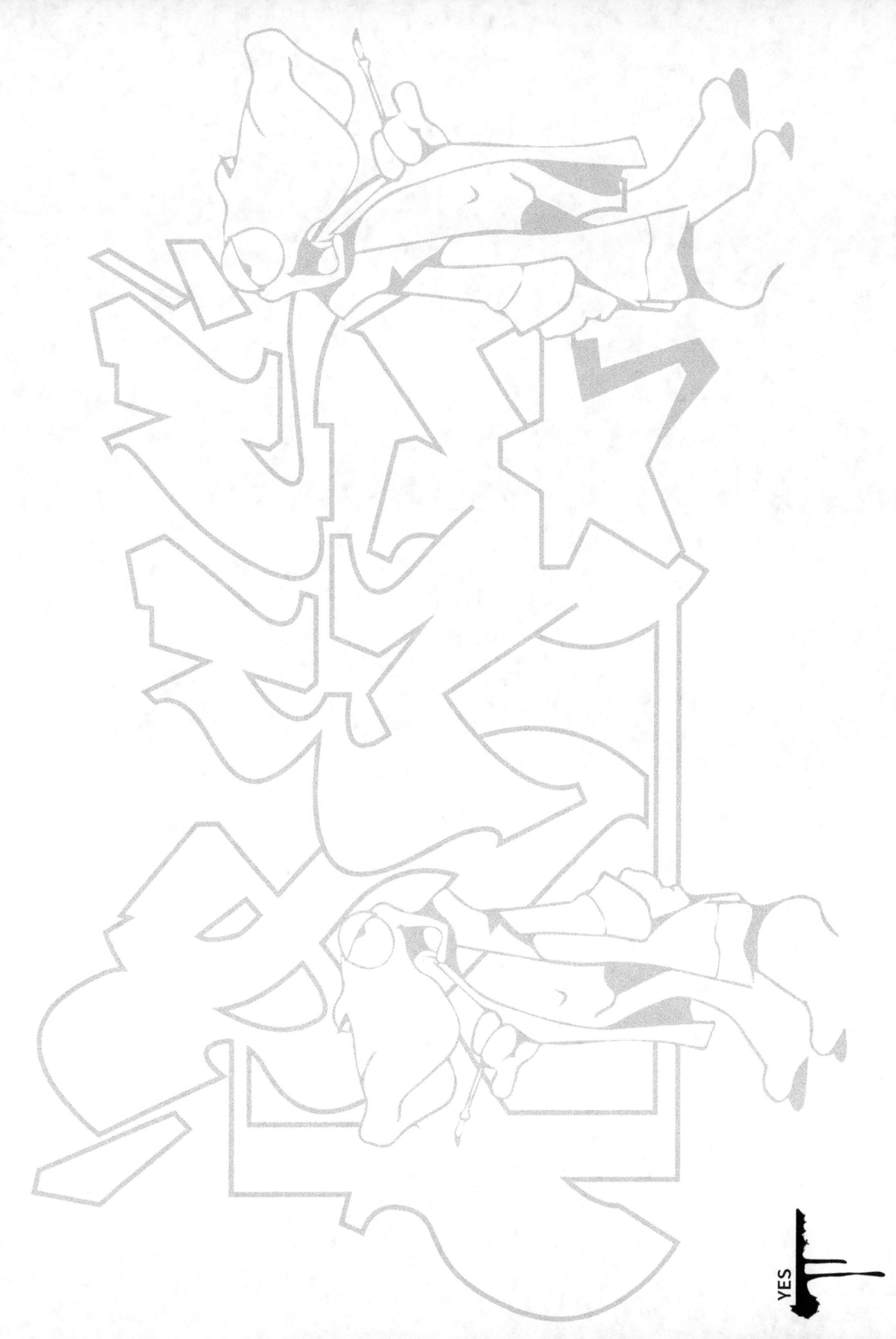

YES

tag the wall

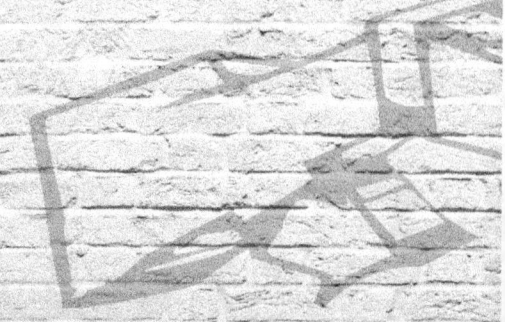

DRAW YOUR OWN BURNER PIECE

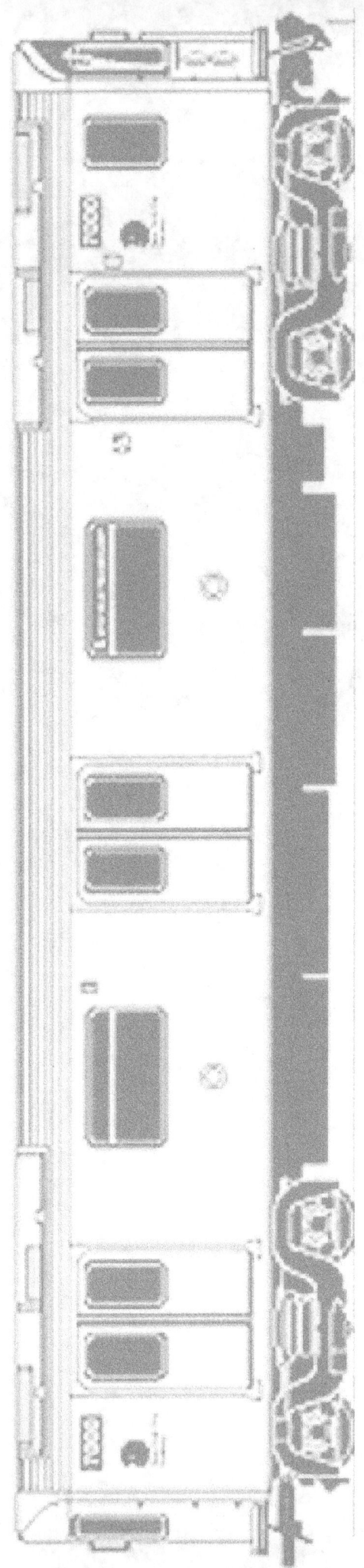

DRAW YOUR OWN TOP-TO-BOTTOM BURNER PIECE

Graffiti Glossary

A Writer's Vocabulary
The following is provided for the use of people outside the writing community.

All-CITY: When a writer or crew bombs all major subway lines or the streets of all five boroughs..
BEEF: Disagreement or conflict.
BENCH: (n) Subway station where writers congregate and watch trains. Benching
        (v) The act of watching trains.
BITE: Plagiarism
BOMB: Prolific writing
BUFF: Removal of writing/art work
BURN: 1. To out do the competition. 2. To wear out.
BURNER: A technically and stylistically well-executed wild style piece. Generally done in bright colors.
CREW: Organized group of writers
CROSSING OUT: To scribble or write on someone else's name. It is considered highly disrespectful.
DEF: Excellent (derived from definite and death).
DOPE: Excellent, of the highest order.
DOWN: Part of a group or action
DT: Plain cloths police officer or detective.
5-O: Slang for police. Derived form the television series Hawaii 5-O.
FADE: Graduation of colors.
GETTING UP: When proliferation of name has led to high visibility.
HIT: (n) A tag, throw-up or piece (v) the act of writing.
IND: NYC subway division called the Independent. Includes A, B, C, D, E, F, GG subway lines.
IRT: NYC subway division called Interborough Rapid Transit. Includes 1, 2, 3, 4, 5, 6, 7, 9 subway lines.
KILL: To bomb excessively.
KING: The most accomplished writer in a given category.
LAY-UP: A single or double track where trains are parked during off-peak hours. Both tunnel
        and elevated lay-ups exist.
MOTION TAGGING: Writing on subway cars while they are in service. Also referred to as MOTIONING
OLD SCHOOL: The writing culture prior to 1984.
        This date can vary greatly depending upon who you ask.
OUTLINE: The skeleton or frame work of a piece FINAL OUTLINE: After fill-in and designs have been
        applied the outline is re-executed to define the letters.
PIECE: A writer's painting, short for masterpiece.
PIECE BOOK OR BLACK BOOK: A writer's sketch book. Used for personal art development and or
        the collection of other artists work.
THE SYSTEM: The New York City Subway system
STYLE WARS: Competition between artists to determine superior creative ability.
TAG: (n) A writer's name and signature. (v) The execution of a signature.
TAGGING-UP: The execution of a signature.
THROW-UP: A quickly executed piece consisting of an outline with or without thin l
        ayer of spray paint for fill-in.
TOP-TO-BOTTOM or (T to B): A piece which extends from the top of the subway car to the bottom.
TOY: Incompetent writer.
WAK: Substandard, terrible.
WRITER: Practitioner of the art of writing.

HELLO
my name is

BlackBook

A Graffiti Coloring Book by: Malcolm Williams AKA King Zoc 5

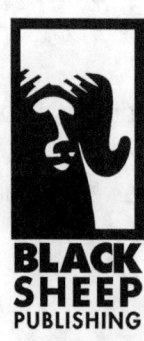

**BLACK
SHEEP**
PUBLISHING